THE SONG
OF
THE COBWEB

Jean Bonnin

...is half French half Welsh. He was born in Lavaur, in the Tarn in France, in the year of the deep snows... He took his first degree in government and politics in Birmingham, and his Masters in political philosophy at Hull; his doctoral research was on the theories of despotism. These days, he is a novelist, poet, graphic designer, artist, and translator of surrealist texts. Specifically, he is the translator of Malcolm de Chazal's Magical Sense (Sense Magique). He is also the inventor of surrealist ping pong...

Through a combination of hard work and serendipity Jean Bonnin has achieved anonymity in New York, Paris, Berlin, London and Wales.
He is a great believer in the following quote by William Burrough's: "The dream is a spontaneous happening and therefore dangerous to a control system set up by the non-dreamers."

Also by Jean Bonnin:

Novels - A Certain Experience of the Impossible; The Cubist's House

Poetry/Aphorisms - Being and Somethingness; Beautiful Wilderness; Dreams Within Dreams; The Bearable Lightness of Being

Translations - Magical Sense (by Malcolm de Chazal); Magical Science (by Malcolm de Chazal)

Edited by Jean Bonnin - The Nuremberg Trials: A Personal History (by Georges Bonnin)
and
Surrealism in Wales; Surrealism in Wales: Artworks and Images

The Song of the Cobweb
An Original Publication of Red Egg
Publishing
First published in the UK in 2022
www.redeggpublishing.com

Copyright © Jean Bonnin 2022

*Jean Bonnin has asserted his moral right to be
identified as the author of this book (only the parts
he has written)*
Cover design: J. Bonnin

British Library Cataloguing-in-Publication Data

A catalogue record for this book is available
upon
request from the British Library
ISBN: 978-1-9998215-8-6

THE SONG OF THE COBWEB

Rimbaud's Last Journey

I am another
With eyes of someone else

It is the eyes that give me
away
Haunted far-off stare

The worried man
Holding it together

As the steps
Of my split
Wooden-heeled soles
Resonate off
The walls of this old
Garrison town

The train will be
Several days late

As I am told this
I bake another
Petrified smile
Above my
Trembling jaw

So I must wait
Wait for the
Goats to clear
The line
Or for repairs to be completed
Or for the driver to sober up
Or for bandits to disband

Whatever it is
I shall buy
Fruit and bread

And water
In French

Await for the locomotive
And follow
In Rimbaud's footsteps

Rimbaud said the air in
Djibouti
Can drive you mad
I say:
Once you've arrived in
Djibouti
It's difficult to leave

The Song of the Cobweb

The cobwebs
Sing
Through
Rain tear droplets' glistening
dust

Light dew morning
Breaks
Over
Sheet-covered furniture

Ghost-like armchair
Filled
With
Ghost-like
Recollections

Memories
Of laughter's
Echoed sorrow
Creak to silence
In our garden's
Fractured overgrowth

Smoking Cigarettes and Talking About Revolution

Smoking cigarettes and talking
about revolution
On peeling wrought-iron
porches
Left over from wicked colonial
times

Rocking and sipping rum
Averting one's gaze from the
sun

Languidly a guitar from a
distance
Oozes through the haze
My mood is the breeze

We have thoughts to change the world
We have ideas that can heel

My ice-cubes become liquid
As I age seamlessly
Gradually absorbed by the ripples in the sky

My rum-glass will refill itself
With a mixture made from liquid regret
As I dream away
These recollections of creeping isolation
Comprised from unfulfilled utopian tomorrows

Forever-land (Pt II)

The empty station's dancing
echo
Reminds me of a desolate
siren
Like meaningless infinity
Or staying at the wrong hotel
with Marlene Dietrich

Like a wildly mythical game of
Forever-land
Filled with footsteps
And the ghosts of women
From Man Ray's photographs

It is the naked train
Within Klaus Kinski

That hurtles us through the wind
Like the ringing of distant pentagrams

But to never arrive
With your packet of Gauloises
And your Gainsbourg smile
Is also something to be admired

For are we not destined always to be
Standing on the wilderness shoreline
Freed from our flames
Listening out for the solitary footstep

Broken Teeth

Today I'll wear a dress
Today I'll cut my throat
Today I'll take a boat
To wear the people's smile
through broken teeth
To where the people smile
through broken teeth

Today I'll speak to the clowns
Today I'll speak to my demons
Today I'll find my friends
Today I'll kill my friends
I have no friends

Tomorrow I'll drink your
poison
Then I shall drink my own

Today I'll buy a gun
Maybe I'll kill someone
Maybe I'll take me a wife
Maybe tomorrow I'll smile
Maybe I'll remember how to smile

Tomorrow I'll take a job
Mow my lawn
Cut some bushes
And sew the dawn

Sometime soon the noises will die
One day soon I'll learn to cry
Close the wounds and fly
Tomorrow I'll comprehend your toxic glue
Tomorrow I'll be the sock inside the stolen shoe

Tomorrow I'll know what to do
I'll kill me or I'll kill you

Don't know what to do

Ripples

Don't sell me snake oil
Pulling over hot coals
With one eye on the rear-view mirror
And one eye on death

Crowns in the desert
Chaos on the deckchairs
Crumbling your architecture
With my notebook in hand

Messages playing backwards
On my vinyl records
Part-time pleasers and firebreathers
And lovers with an axe to grind

Ripples in the timeframe
Playing another boardgame
How I wish
Things could be the way they were

The sun is falling
And the rain is shining
How I wish
Things could be the way they were

Don't sell me snake oil
Pulling over hot coals
With one eye on the rear-view mirror
And one eye on death

People at Bus-stops

Faces
And places
And indiscriminate traces
Numbers on houses
And worn-out shoes
People at bus-stops
The occasional nut-job
Kentucky wrappers
Finger-licking chatters
Skyping and jibing
And birthday cake piping
From the last baker's shop
In the town
Populist slogans
And racist overtones
From people with confidence

Who are indifferent about
providence
Or of history repeating itself

Or of history repeating itself

Tonight

Tonight
Tonight I will drink
I will drink to live
And to die
I will drink
For all the poets
Who grapple
For my hand in the darkness
So they too can live and die

Tonight
Tonight I shall smoke
Smoke the way that hobos do
I shall smoke to all the days
And the nights
And the unhurried afternoons

When we were going to live
forever

And I shall love
I shall love the way
When it never used to matter
And yet it mattered more
Than all the stars floating
In my mug of whiskey

And then I shall play the
Pogues
And we shall dance
In that flailed madness
Of delirious beauty
That only
Trapped broken-winged
Moments
Of freedom can breath

Ricochets

Maybe madness has taken
Your mind
You've been singing songs
For an audience
Of misfits
All for the appreciation
Of strangers
When all you'd really rather do
Is make sandcastles
On a deserted
Southern beach
And await the ricochets
To hit the church bell
For a final time

But instead
You wipe

Your brow
As you nod and bow
And feel like a tin of sardines
And you really must
Get that crack in the ceiling fixed
As you're subsiding
And gliding
And sliding
Into the deep waters
Of another
Impenetrable day

Chants on Circling Wings

Your breath chants through meadows
Whispering in the silent languages
Once rumoured long ago

Daybreak over mountains and hilltops
Catches on wings
Circling towards the distant abyss

Our hollow adventures will soon
Be forgotten
And placed alongside
Other equally

Foolhardy Priorities

Fourteen days of Eating Only Rice

My mirror is
the
teardrop
of infinity

Reflecting
silence
and
ravaged
solitude

The clouds
provide
solace

As the

breeze
propels
them
to where
the mirrors
dare not go
      and piles them up
      into cloud
      mountains
      with rivers
      of snow

Where the
sunshine-mind
can play
freely
as it
awaits
yesterday's laughter
to arrive

Woman on a Train

The woman on the train
Thought about moonlight on
the sea
Wishing for another life

In her mind
Droplets of molten moonlight
Sizzled on contact with the
waves

Like dreams
The train continued
Through the silver lit
mountains

Her head bobbing gently
against the window

She knew she could never return
Not to the life she'd led

Alone in the carriage
She opened the window
And breathed in the unfamiliar air

She gathered her belongings
Coat, hat, keys, passport, bank cards,
Bag, neckless, blouse and wig

She threw them from the train window
Watched as they fleetingly scattered and bounced
She took her dress off and unfolded her jeans

She threw the dress from the window
Put on the jeans, washed her face
And was then ready for a new life

The Doll's Last Stand

The infinite
Knocks on the door
The balloon wanders past
The bottom of my garden
The mirror she stroked
Caught my reflection
Yet showed that I was another
We drank through the night
To the fire and the doll's last
stand
All the surrounding trees
Breathed their bowed
enormity
Amidst the invisible silence
Of never-ending happenstance
Love laughed and playfully
danced

In the knowledge that
Everything was going to be
alright

Everything was going to be
alright

Glue and Old Paper

The envelopes squeezed under
the door
Rest silently upon the doormat
Virgin white and pre-war
brown
But to read them would
destroy them
Destroy their mystery

They announce a death
A love, an apology
The manifestation of a bored
moment
Or a forced desire to continue
a relationship
That should long-since have
ceased to be

She crouches naked
Upright, foetal
On the balls of her feet

She does not wish to die
She wishes to fade away
To be forgotten
Forgotten and forget

To fade away completely
Breath, live, dance on the inside
In a vacuum
Of imaginary walls
Where no sound can enter or leave

She wishes to float
To hover with no name
To be an un-opened letter

Simultaneously both dead and alive
On the edge of meaning

The Surrealist Artist

He pirouettes around meaning
Indefinable in his precision
Love, movement, sunset, nature
Days and nights merge
Into a poetry of light and shade and colour
Rooted in the beautiful mystery
Of alchemy and time
He portrays the femininity
Of the androgyny
Of the legends and magic
In the glimpses of silhouettes
From the corners of eyes
Caught with whispers
As the passing clouds

Consider his meaning
Caressed moments
From when we blink ourselves
Absorbing and absorbed
Into the mesmerising poetry
Of the next reality
Of the beyond reality
Of sur-reality

Settling

Have you seen it
The way the clouds
Talk with silence

Have you seen the living
The way their eyes
Are imploring

Have you taken the time
To fathom out
How our dreams are stolen

Have you wondered
About poetry
And answers

Have you felt

The splashing waves
Sting the tears on your cheeks

Has life flowed
In and out
Like the rhythm of the waves

And have you been soothed
By how the moon
Settles our yearning

Drink The Sky

The lunatics laugh
Mad shattered scattered
Laughter
As if knowledge is their final
weapon
Secrets in the darkness
For us to discover
And uncover from
Realms
That only a few have visited
Lonely souls
Whose only friends
Are silence and dreams
And the forgotten tomorrows
Of enforced solitude

It is lonely up here - drink the
sky!

Wichita Confessions

My red balloon got lost in the tree
The tree was lost in the desert
The desert was lost on the island
The island was lost in the ocean
The ocean was lost between continents
The continents were lost on the globe
The globe was lost in the solar system
The solar system was lost in the universe
The universe was lost in space
The space was inside my head

The Dying Day

The tree and mirror fracture
my streets from the drip drip
raincoat diagnostics that
collar-up my laugh at the
throngs of statue towers'
indifference to motel murders
and holes in walls from the
neon gunshot ricochet where I
burn my old self in a bathroom
that has seen better days
emerging from solace
crystalline chrysalis laughing
out of pointed shoes and
strong coffee taxi cab awaiting
the sudden re-direction of
parallel thoughts cluttering for
prominence on schizophrenic

mornings which became
afternoons before the leaf falls
in the alleyway and makes the
dying day into a poem.

Religion

May your porcelain gods
tumble and crack
May your clay jesuses be
trampled under foot
Your lines of trees are sentry
soldier men
Upright, distinguished,
awaiting their demise
May you indeed throw away
your chains
To replace them with
handcuffs and an iron bit
Your flowers are weeds
As your affection rotten and
decayed
Slashing beauty with your
tongues of fear

Your control and lies
And your abhorrence of love
Drip dripping purified water
From your putrefied well

Yet poetry and dreams
Shall always defeat your angels
of death

Love Stroked to the Infinite

I laughed
that I
was trees
    breathed
through
    everything

In
the knowledge that
    everything
inhales
amidst invisible
playful dance

    Love
stroked
    to

   the infinite
     knocks on the door
and lowers its voice

The bowed
enormity
   knocks once more
     and
shows us
     everything
through the reflection
   of dreams
on lost trains

Space
   breathed

  I
  drank
through

the invisible silence
of
never ending stories
   exhaled

   Love
  laughed
bowed
and stroked
to the
infinite

The Death of the Poet

The death of the poet
Stopped the trains
The king spoke from his
sickness bed
But no one believed him

The death of the poet
Meant that the hope
Had been stifled
Love extinguished

The death of the poet
Was a mysterious event
An accident
Was the official line

The poet's death

Was in a darkened room
Unvisited
And untouched

The poet sat alone
Safe for a candle
Parchment
And pen

His death was unexpected
At the height of his powers
Is what had been said
Before... before... before

The solitary trickle
That traced a line along the
contours of his wrinkles
Was the consistency of his
Indian Ink
But it was not ink

The door was locked
On the inside
When they found him
His final action of defiance

The slumped head
The crossed arms
The final poem
From what would turn out to
be the final poet
When they moved him
And were able to read
His final message to those who
he still
Deep-down believed loved him
It read:

I tried. I tried so hard
I tried… I tried and I failed

Desolate Distraction

Desolate distraction
Because sounds are
sometimes more
More than
More than those echoes from
past crossroads
Crossroads
Crossroads I regret
I regret having believed
Having believed I was never
going to regret

Memories shout and whisper
LOUD and silent
The chaos of now
Now shouts
And is gone

Grasp it
Before it becomes something
To look back on

A door slams
A car backfires
Inconsequential
Not to them
Possibly also to them
Possibly not

Weave our overlaps
To create another
Lane of spaghetti
Another
Highway
To look
Back on
Another door
To slam

Or
To open wide

Grab the overlaps
Till they
Go blue
In the face
Do the sudden thing
Not the thought-out thing
Shake the moment
Jolt the now
Jolt the now
Electrify it
Make it fizz
Make it sizzle
Make it heat up

Burn
Burn strong into the night
And then cool down

Cool down
Cool it right down
Cold as ice
Easy now
Go for a midnight swim
Drown the regret
And grab the moment

For Dream Melody

When I thought of the dream
Within the dream
I heard a splendid resonation

I awoke and flung the fantasy
Into a kingdom full of
nightmares

Then once
Upon a midnight magic
I sat
Engaged and sleeping

And on that day
My soul grew charmed

Dreaming

I dreamed you were dreaming
Of a dream I once had
For we are but memories
Of thoughts we never had

I dreamed that you were dreaming
Of the people we once were
Laughing, singing and dancing
And then we'd disappear

I dreamed that I was dreaming
Dreaming that I was awake
Sitting in the sunshine
And swimming naked in the lake

I dreamed I was laughing
From beyond my sleep
How time and space are imagined
And how a day feels like a week

I dreamed that I was dead again
Snoring silent prose
Taping up my mouth
And clasping tight my nose

For the end shall come one day
And with it new reverie
For experience is a circle
Inside which we see what we choose to see

My Kissing T-shirt

I'm wearing my black kissing t-shirt once again
Feeling like a troubadour requiring more elbow room

Optimism is spelt within the crumples
Of its cotton black defence

The shop window stops me
With its broken 'closed' sign
Doubled-up manikins
Old pendulum timepieces
And Bakelite dreams
From a future
That was never realised

I stand there for far too long
From inquiring to
uncomfortable
Within the strike of a chime
From the half-hearted cuckoo
On the reflected far wall...
My own reflection is streaked
Within the drizzled stains
Of the window pane

I sense I've been lumped in
With those lonely socially
awkward souls
By the woman across the
street
But I'm not that... I'm more
More simply unsure (of
myself)

I seem to be constantly on the look out
For things that don't exist
Yet that almost do exist
That should exist...
That are so close to being real
It almost hurts
Since only I get it

Everything should exist
Every possible thought
Whether it's 'true',
Whatever that is, or not
- like my kissing t-shirt

Banners and Flags

Don't let them in
Marching over the hill
With their banners and their flags
And their stupid beliefs

Don't let them in
Before they destroy everything
Black shirts and pointed horns
Baseball hats and racist tunes

Stop them in their tracks
Don't let truth get in the way
Of alternative facts
Stop them in their tracks

You're being manipulated

Puppets on a string
Right wing masters
Laughing up their sleeves

And rushing off to the bank
Pulling the strings
To make the desperate sing
While rushing off to the bank
And manipulating everything

It's The Rain

It's the rain I tell you
It's the rain
The rustle of the trees
On melancholic evenings

It's the rain I tell you
That adds to my feelings
Props up my fear and loathing
Dripping down my face and my ceiling

Then when it clears
The light is more silvery
And some of the puddles
Have petrol rainbows

One of my shoes

Has a hole in it
Only a small hole
Maybe it is a metaphor

It's the rain I tell you
Sucking me in, blowing me out
Makes me who I am
Full of optimism and doubt

Rain… rain… rain
Bring on the rain

Smiling its terrified

drink
  the forgotten tomorrows
Of
     enforced solitude

It is
the lonely souls
who
only
    a few have visited

    Lonely souls
Who have visited
    Mad shattered solitude

It
 is

the lonely
    souls who
have visited
the
splintered
laughter of
    frightened knowledge

Who
 drink up
the darkness
   for
us to discover

As if
   knowledge is
unfulfilled tomorrows
   Of enforced scattered
solitude

Days break
As
    Daybreak
Swings around
Another corner
    Smiling its terrified
   deFiant
Glare
  As though
Nothing has happened

•

Still Life

The polished apple
Faces us, green and russet
The grapes, a large bunch of
bruised burgundy
Are the focal point
An off-round Chinese
grapefruit
Five kiwis positioned in a
contrived haphazard fashion
And four bananas that have
been misguidedly
Placed around the edges of the
shallow ceramic bowl
To create the effect of an
attendant
Carmen Miranda headpiece

A painter
If indeed any painter
Would waste her time on such
a deformity
Should call her work
The Gorilla's Embrace

17 Cisterns

I thought about 17 cisterns
Parrots and wrist-rooms
Fences and teardrops
Amalgamated and alchemy

Then I thought about you

I chose license plates
Caught too late
Ray-gun phase and immortal dress
Eyebrow pencil and melted teacher

Then I thought about you

Knee-high to a lunatic

Androgenous metamorphosis
Note pads of flapping wings
Everyone dances and everyone sings

Then I thought about you

Understand water caves
Making lipsticks into halves
Wish I'd thought of that before
Rain plummeting to the floor

Then I thought about you

Reflections on a Berlin Tram

I rode the Berlin tramway
With Bowie in my ears
Trying to recreate the time
When he and Iggy
Played charades with life and death

Popping pills and popping thrills
Drinking beer and eating air

My reflection
A four-eyed freak
Looking back at me
From a universe
Where all faces are deformed
By the melting by terror

Of public scrutiny and anomie

My shortsightedness
Jumbled with variegated
flashes
Of circus mirror mis-direction
Cloud my perception

Is she staring at me
Or also idly listening to Bowie
Wishing industrial resonances
And crumbling concrete
certitudes
Would return

If only for one day

I turn to glance in her direction
She manoeuvres her gaze
away

Misfortunate coincidence
Or a sign of troubled solitude

I wish my freak train reflection
would turn and laugh at me

She alights at the next stop
She stands still, sideways-on
And lights a cigarette
She inhales and exhales before
turning to smile at me
Our eyes, as with our cross-
eyed doubles, hold still
For a moment that is longer
Than for there to have been no
meaning at all
...And then she walks away

Flows Life Pass

Duck bone
Metronome
Ticking life
Streams

Chip shop Charlie
Mary's at the Party
With the ladies
From the Asher-lee set

Artist intolerant
Revolutionary solvent
Gluing ourselves
Together

Summer city dust
Flows life pass

When hope sidles
Backwards

The rainbows are plexiglass
Hoover time for Mr Shine
Everest waiting in line
We are tranquil summits

Peak Me

I was feeling down
Happening on nowhere to stay
Been running around
But not wanting to play

Staring at the clouds
Hoping it's gonna rain
Enjoying my mood
Happy with my level of pain

Stars gather around my thoughts
Making me wish for improbable things
I'm younger than I feel
But older than I want to be

I judge a poem
By the shape of someone's mouth
A look in their eyes
And a fire in their heart

I'll arrive at the middle
When I'm finished with the start
I'm feeling strong and sounding weak
It won't be long before I'm past my peak

Standing at a bus-stop
Waiting for a taxi which looks like a train
The skies have split open
… I think it's going to rain

The Knelt Tree

the tree fracture goes screams
from the drip drip
bieldier that collar-up my
laugh at the throngs of statue
forest indifference to murders
and holes in walls from the
neon gunshot demanded
brave motel seclusion lips go
old wild if a bathroom that has
seen my burnt days identity
identify from comate
crystalline chrysalis laughing
out of bedraggled hobo shoes
and scrags of a taxi man
around the sudden re-
direction parallel thoughts
under-breath sniggerers for

prominence on schizophrenic mornings which become afternoons before the hues of Potemkin village from intertie making the knelt die into a poem.

Hands In Pocket

My hands are in my pocket
They would like to swing
By my side
If they could

I am in a field
In Wiltshire
Having visited
A friend

Stone circles
Remind me
Of night-time dances

The sun and I squint
At each other
Hazy mist

Time is irrelevant
There is no time
No time
Time

Floating Thoughts

I'm constantly trying to
capture something
The feel of waves and wind
and tranquil dislocation
The way a seagull feels on
currents of air
The way the sea spray stings
my cheeks

My laughter floats away to
other planets
To one day be registered
On the instruments of alien
ghosts from alien lands
Where I shall never hear my
laughter again

Down here the waters swell
and splash
The rocks sing out
As the chrome sky
Washes curious contentment
over my weary distractedness

A solitary ray of sun
Briefly shines down and then
dissolves
As if summoning me to return
To the laughter I once knew

Yet I feel natural and at home
In this environment with the
moon and the cliffs
And the breeze as it whispers
Through the creaking bows of
time

Immortal Solutions

I'm too wired to switch off my mind
Too tired to sleep
Too alive to die
Too much money in people's eyes

I'm going to have to become immortal
To solve all of these problems

Here comes another summer of hope
Of Berlin roses and beautiful jungles
Here comes another summer of expectation

Waiting for a revolution,
waiting for change

Speeding all night and
snoozing all day
Too sleepy to register
Too dumbstruck to speak out
Too many jobs to be done
Too much concrete replacing
the fun

Catching a Breath

I wish I'd timed it better
All the joy
All the dreams
Paced myself
Staggered my life
Saved some for later
Not to have packed so much
Into such few moments
She said it would go on forever
So then you relax
You've got all the time in the world
I don't have to catch hold
Of these beautiful moments in my hands
For there will be another one
Along in a moment

And then another one after that

Catching a breath
In an airtight
Transparent container
Kept on a mantlepiece
Yet with the folding of time
You forget why you did it
Its importance
The feeling you had
But she did say it would go on forever

Spirals of Primordial Interconnected Isolation

Below the warm reaches of
the sun's gaze
The beginning...
I channel meditational waves
Into weaves of dreams and
memories of the future, as yet
unsung
The intertwining of spirits with
my courage and my hopes

Other perceptions from other
worlds, my worlds, our shared
worlds
I assemble to create new
realities, both within reach and
just out-of-touch

Time evaporates into the
morning mists of half-glimpsed
other realities
That echo the newly learnt
slowness of my heart
Which mirror the never-ending
days

I proceed – under the shade of
the fig tree until time grasps at
my thoughts
Telling me to stand back, take-
in, appreciate
Reflection and thought
travelling along with the
particles

I conclude just in time

Before the storm eats up the
silence of my heart
Growls at me for daring to lose
myself
In flashes that have seemed
like one solitary unbroken
moment

The drips become drops
As the sky covers over
Creating patterns and dimness
It is the sign for me to finish.

A Trip to Cardigan

Mae Bird sits like chocolate
upon cream
Glinting nose stud upon our
dream
Conversation is film as rain
becomes sandwich
All surrealists roll sideways
when drinking from rivers

The smell of freshly baked
soda bread
Dances on my salivation glands
Like a black bird hopping
In a pool of tear shaped ball
bearings

He said that he'd escort poetry

Disguised as a book
I had nothing to give
Safe for stories about disguises

The rain sucked up the spirit
And made summer seem
Further than it had ever been
My nose is a carrot

This exercise of luxury hot
chocolates
And hidden meanings
Will no doubt be repeated
All radiators are on the blink in
Cardigan

On leaving I visited the woman
with the crystals
She is fun and looked cold
I shall re-tread all my footsteps

For the warmth of the
Apache's tears

Snow and Keroscene

No more concrete
And no more soldiers below
my feet
Sunset adoption
With a cigarette and a potion
Raising a glass to the times
when I had to steal my beers

Violin nights under a
saxophone moon
Light a violet candle, I'll be
home soon

My boots are sodden and my
raincoat's tawdry
Whistling my way along, cos
I've nothing more to say

The snow and the kerosene
Melting my optimism on
another late-night scene
Pour another drink and stare
like a lunatic
Rattling my ice-cube, cos I'll be
home soon

And as my early morning shoes
Drag my heels towards the
hills
I light-up and smile my only
smile
Cos I know I'll be home soon

Throat On My Back

Rattle down the track
I can feel
The throat on my back

Hobo hitching
With my
Porcupine hat

Love and jellyfish
I've become a membrane
Alone on a train

Morning sun
Peel away
Behind the mountain

Hanging on

Dozing down
Desert sand sound

Endless timeless
Rattle down the track
I am free

I am free
I have brought along
My mind for company

A Burning Heart

I wish I could bury all your
words
Throw them away
Forget them
Burn them on top of a high
mountain

Incendiary amnesia
Lit from a burning heart

Cut out the memories
With a scalpel
And wait for your superficial
beauty
To decay

Blinded by my Best Friend's Hat

You and your elastic leggings and your comedy heaven. Reflections of tofu and pomegranate seeds. Considerations for table football decks. The days of furry dice have been replaced by the inevitable recorded buzzes of the bumblebee. As a montage background to eat premium muffins on a Chinese plate with a salad leaf for £14.25. Track down hypnosis around the corner. The Fish and Chip Wars are a heavy load ... Blinded by my best friend's hat ... while reading fanatics and collectors watching someone show off with a big car, little brain and a loud hi-fi system playing something out of a mid-eighties non-descriptive musical history. Angered by the words he does not understand; it must be a conspiracy against the middle classes. I used to watch The Tube on Friday night before going out with black eyeliner, a belly full of expectations, and pointy shoes. Yell!!!!

Pirouette Around Meaning
II

We pirouette around Meaning

to indefinable
precision

We pirouette
through the movement of
trees
       through our
   handcuffed
    identity

We pirouette around meaning
        around
meaning

We pirouette around meaning
    Our
   tumble and talking

   Dancing to indefinable
precision

   The
movement of
   trees sway to the
movement   of love

   Dance to
 indefinable
precision
   Moving to our indefinable
precision
 of trees through
   the winds
of our meaning

Duchamp's Paranormal Goblet

George Best wore a vest
Made from the tears from
Duchamp's goblet

Chess pieces move themselves
In the caves of 'endless giving'

Time takes a cigarette and
flicks it in the air
Major Tom juggles clouds and
catches them in his hair

Cod war cod piece Miro's
wearing a three-piece

The virgin Mary is getting
leery, said the donkey to the
clown

And the lunatics will soon take
over
So at last we'll get some sense
round here

All of which makes me feel
Paranormal in The Preselis
Holding hands with a game of
Risk
And the exquisite Patti Smith

The Last Poet

The last ever poet
Sat in her rocking chair
In the middle of a field

Soon they would come for her
As they had come for the
others
She had to be stopped

She created castles out of air
A single flower in an eternal
desert
And life from death

She gave meaning to the
hidden words
Invented new colours

Dulled the pain of love
And constructed paradise
Out of cosmic flames

But beauty and comprehension
And the melding together of contradictions
Were no longer required
In the new time

Her field was so beautiful
With trees and mountains and waterfalls
Yet her layered horizon both imagined and real
Could not wish away her impending fate

Glances Untitled

crystal glance through prismed
departures
    Your dream
  Glinting
nose stud
upon
cream

  Smiled crystal glances pass
the drinking of soft wings and
the river stations

    To
  the breath

Glinting
from river's

breath
    Glinting of soft
winds

    As we
acknowledge
    the memory
        that
  reminds us of who
  we
  used to
be
    As smiled
    crystal glances pass
by

 The
call of
  our recollection
  comes as the

tide has turned

youth reminds
　us of flocked longing

　　Nudged significances pass
the rivers
　of oak
　　　For Cardigan is film as
　　　rain becomes sandwich

Divinely imperfect

Strangle me in your
effervescent glow
Love of chaos
And jumble dance light swirls
Your spirit
Moulded from distant light
Shoots past my skylight
On its journey to the moon

Silver webs on rain-glistened
morning
Vibrating in the gentle breeze
Like prisms of pyramids
Shattering light into its
component parts
So I have become a child

Held tight in the presence of magic

Electricity comes from other planets
Your power is unknown to you
Breathing sparks into the flames
Sunlight in the shadows
And paintings onto the walls of caves
You are the immortality of tribal chants

Divinely imperfect
Beautifully ambiguous
A creature of legend and myth

My Friend Discovered Jesus
(alternate version from song)

My friend discovered Jesus
And now I'm
    going
    to telephone the devil

    It made his window get
stoned
While he listened to my
telephone

I filmed the Devil

I filmed the Devil
    As my friend
      was discovering Jesus

In the universe

In the universe
   he's found
      Jesee-verse
Cheese-ee-verse

Through the
  Devil
My
friend discovered Jesee-verse

   Listen to telephones with
everything
As I filmed the Devil
He discovered Jesus

Then he filmed
the
Devil ... and discovered
he recovered
and telephoned himself

Melting Memories

Piano
Melted delicately
Over meadows of our
forgotten youth

Sunshine's
Hazy descent
Through the woods where we
used to play

Memories
Buttoned up tight
As protection from the sorrow
and regret

Laughter
At the joy

Of never-ending sun-drenched days

Tears
Over lost moments
For all the experiences
That our decisions
Prevented us from having

Thanks for reading this. I hope you enjoyed it...

And thanks to Red Egg Publishing for publishing this collection of my poems.

More of the same and different can be found on my website:
www.jeanbonnin.com
                    Jean Bonnin
                    20-01-22

We are Red Egg Publishing
www.redeggpublishing.com

www.ingramcontent.com/pod-product-compliance
Lightning Source LLC
Chambersburg PA
CBHW060201050426
42446CB00013B/2930